Eighteen

Straight

Whiskeys

ISBN No.: 0-9658674-0-4

Second Printing – September, 2003

The Bowery Press
New York, New York

Printed in the U.S.A.

Thank you: Keith, Stewart - my blood. For being like a brother, Kamar. My "Family of Friends"—Darrell, Chris T., Mike C., Daniel, Tamara, Peter, David, Dan C., Chris R., Dave, Kindall, Rex, Shaun, Carrie, Kristine, Dyrk, Sean W., Rob M. — *To all of you "May life be a martini before and a cigarette after..."*

To Joan, for her love and kindness... For gig, life and word advice: Michael S., Billy M., Bruce, Wings H., David L., John S.Y., Stephen J.C. ...The Lacoix family for their spare room in Paris, summer 1994, where much of this book was written.

Influence and Inspiration: Jack Kerouac, Jimi Hendrix, Raymond Carver, John Cassavetes, Charles Bukowski, Van Morrison, Sam Shepard, Miles Davis, Joan Didion, Brendan Behan, Joe Strummer, Robert Johnson, Dylan Thomas, Henry Rollins, Charles Baudelaire, Eddie Vedder, Leonard Cohen, Trent Reznor, Dave Alvin, Federico Garcia Lorca, Bob Dylan, Ornette Coleman...*You have kept this soul afloat.*

Contents

for my mother
who left too soon.

Eighteen Straight Whiskeys

Michael Easton

THE BOWERY PRESS
NEW YORK, NEW YORK

ONE

*"I had eighteen straight whiskeys.
I think that's the record."*

— Dylan Thomas' last words.

Exits

*even death will have exits
like a dark theatre.*
—Charles Bukowski

Didn't die.

Couldn't of died in that car crash
playing his sax on speed.

Thirty smiles says he didn't die.

Cause he could sleep on concrete
and rest well.
Knew all the bus routes from L.A. to T.J.

Didn't die cause we need him to say,
"Give me a minute, I'm just a little tired of fighting"

He never died the times before.
When he hit the wife's car
pulling into the garage drunk one night
—he didn't die.
Didn't die when she left him.

Dying was never part of the gig.
Cause he'd fall down stairs
and climb to his feet. Laughing.

In time, he was gonna win the lottery.
Still see him walking in the rain
with his broken umbrella open talking about it.

The man was a prince.
Not in a Charles and Diana kinda way—
more like, *royalty in exile.*
He had deeper thoughts in the think,
than the rest of us riff raff. . .

Besides, he was a bartender.
The real thing—
one that knows more about Kierkegard than herpes.

Couldn't of died.
Cause he hated "Lifestyles of the Rich and Famous."
Read a dog earred Jack Kerouac back to the front.
Listened to Jimi—
used to play "Little Wing" over and over
on his horn.

Didn't die cause he'd already been to Hell
about a million times. Always enjoyed his stay.

Not then, not now.

He's just resting.
Holed up in some roadside motel,
drinking J.D., waiting for the sun to come up
and a bus to pass his way.
Then he'll get up.

Come back.

Clean

The guy in the stall next to me
is in bad shape.
I hear him snort some coke,
then he pukes.

Barf splashes onto my shoes.
And as I look down I hear him moan
and talk.
Toilet words.

Into the porcelain,
low and hollow. Begging.
Oh God! Oh God!
And even though he puked on my shoes,
I feel for him.

Been clean for sixty three days.
Full on pasta, not shit.
Just sitting on a toilet,
and thinking there's a poem in this —
somewhere.

A poem about this guy doubled
over the tank, and me
thinking about myself,
with barf on my shoes.

Hearing his friends outside the john,
shouting at him.
Calling him Manson, because
his name is Charles.
And laughing.

Laughing at their drunk, stoned friend.
Laughing at the way he can't hold it anymore.

Wanting to leave this place.
Knowing if I go home now
and write this poem,
without a bottle in front of me,
it will be different.

Without being so drunk, that I might
even be able to read what I wrote
in the morning.
Yes I think, hurry home.
This is going to take some time.

Love Letter

Ink on drink rings. For you.
I know that doesn't mean very much.
Yes, I'm still trying to get this out of my system.
It's dark out and I'm thinking of us.

Nights have been bad lately, worse than usual.
Staring at pills and Red Label and waiting
for sleep to come.
In the pitch; remembering a time when I thought
we still had something.
If something is being too drunk to get out
of bed sometimes.

Staying at that place by the beach,
making love and listening to your tapes all day.
Bizet. Verdi. Puccini.

Do you know that I miss you?
How can you? You're not reading words right now —
you're lying in bed, next to someone else.
Some guy who would never play Ornette Coleman
records during sex. That's why you're happy now.

Don't ask me how I know these things.

And yes, I'm still bartending, if it matters.
But in a four star hotel this time.
Erase that—you're probably staying in one.
I always knew you could. With your looks.
Your ways.

So why did I love you? So much.
How did I ever say goodbye?
Did I say goodbye or is that my lie?
Maybe you walked out on me. I always forget.

Did you explain everything in a letter marked PERSONAL?
I never got it.
Maybe you wrote something after a shower in the steam
of the bathroom mirror. I missed it.
Miss everything but stumble through.

I just keep wondering if this is us?
Can we borrow some hope somewhere,
or is this the way it will be forever?

Ink on drink rings again. For you.

Paradise, California

This place where Raymond Carver lived for awhile.
A place ten miles north of Chico,
that offered low cost housing for his family.
He enrolled in beginning creative writing at Chico State.
This man who wrote stories and poems
and talked with Bukowski.
He said every poem is a love poem.
This place, Paradise, California
where he might of done some fishing,
meant nothing to me before
but now it seems significant,
because Raymond Carver lived there for awhile.

Hands

The man, needed to seduce other women
besides the mom I mean. And when
she caught on, which she always did,
he would try to charm her.
He could charm anyone, the dad.

He'd bring home a bottle for them,
and a new dress for her, and they'd dance
in the kitchen, playing Etta James records
which the mother liked.

The boy would just watch.
Watch the father's big hands resting firmly
in place around her waist, holding her
like the spoiled child he was.

Hands that always scared the boy.
The hands he once saw lift up the back
of a dune buggy out in the desert.
Hands he remembered telling his friends about in school
and they thought his dad was cool.

What the boy didn't tell his friends, was how
on that same trip to the desert, he saw those hands
break the mother's nose.

Not knowing which one exactly, maybe the left.
The right hand was usually quiet,
he never used it for more than holding a cigarette
or lifting a beer.

Cause it was the left one, that when
the yelling began, directed the boy to go stand
on the other side of the sand dune,
away from the camp.

And the son ran and sat and watched
the shadows change across the sand.
He saw a snake, but wasn't afraid
and it passed, like time, nearby.

He began to dream of other places, when he heard
the scream. He started to climb the hill, slowly
sliding down into the hot desert sand.
Climbing, until he was able to look out
over the dune.

And he saw the dad sitting on his motorcycle,
revving his bike loudly, then taking off down the road
over some hills and disappearing.

The mother came out of the trailer
and sat in the door step. A handkerchief
covered part of her face and she was crying.
Bloodstains, on the front of her new dress.

He ran to her, her body shaking
and her head tilted back. He moved slowly,
put his arms around his mother's waist
and when his hands came together he locked them
and held her, as tight as he possibly could.

Elmer Fudd

You're waiting for her to go cocktail,
so you can lie around in your boxers,
drink beer and eat rolls.
A good night to watch the lawn grow.
Waiting to have the place to yourself,
so you can glance through her Cosmopolitans
and booze the bit up.
Waiting to watch a ball game.
Any ball game, it doesn't matter.
Just waiting to get to watch what you
want to watch. Jeopardy and cartoons.
The old kind of cartoons without all the robots
and space shit. Good ones.
Like Bugs Bunny and Elmer Fudd.
Dig Elmer Fudd.
Waiting to watch reruns.
Sanford and Son. Get Smart. The Three Stooges.
Waiting for Moe and Larry and Curly.
Not Shep. If it's Shep you'll go back to
the cartoons—even if they are the space ones.

Waiting to put the V.C.R. to some use.
Accidentally erase the tape with her Soaps on it.
Waiting to forget to tape "Knott's Landing."
How can she watch that crap anyway?
Besides, you'll be watching "On the Waterfront"
at the time. That you're sure of—

Maybe fix that clogged toilet
and some other things, if you have the time.
Waiting.
Waiting for her to go so you can get
to all this stuff.

And then you see her,
packs her purse with all that junk
she carries around with her.
Runs out the door, late as always.
And you sit. Motionless.
For quite some time.

Wondering how much longer,
she's going to stay with you
and your ways.

Hope

We were very good at hope, my wife and I.
We hoped for twins.
A boy, his name would be Jeff.
A girl, her name would be Laura.

We hoped for this right up until
they wheeled my wife into the delivery room.
She waved at me as she passed down the corridor
and I was left to wait and hope in my room
alone. And I started to hope for other things
so I could be good to Laura and Jeff.

An important job, one with good money,
so some day I could buy a car that was new.
And a V.C.R. And so maybe that
Speigel catalogue that my wife is always looking at
over at her sister's, would come to our house as well.
Be able to look at an entire catalogue of things
to hope for. So I was surprised to see our
doctor standing in the doorway of the room
where I waited.

He said there were complications,
tried to settle me, then left.

Darkness passing,
while crying and praying are the same.
Counting moments till sometime that morning.
The doctor that speaks slowly,
explaining what has been done.

In her room I knelt and kissed
her swollen cheek, she tried to smile.
We held hands, my head at her side
and remained still for a time, together.

When I looked up, I realized we'd never
hope for anything again.

Paradise

> *I still dwelled deep in my elected paradise*
> *—a paradise whose skies were the color of*
> *hell flames—but still a paradise.*
>   - Vladamir Nabokov, *Lolita*

She tears him apart.
The way she holds back,
pulls her punches,
forgets her lies.
The way she'll spit in the fountain
while he makes his wish.
And laugh.

She goes out on him, blatantly.
Disregards their lunch dates
and embarrasses him in front
of his associates.
Likes to drink Stoli,
and do lines.
Says, "Blah, Blah, Blah"
Alot.

Butterflies won't land on her.
And still he loves her.

So he calls me
in the middle of the night.
Crying into the phone.
Just cries, without a "Hello."
This man who went to college
and fixes teeth.
Who finds himself on a pay phone
at a lousy hour, desperate
and looking for her.

He's breathing heavy and coughs often.
Tells me about the crazy thoughts
that have passed over him lately,
"Misguided," is the word he uses.
Says that he hasn't slept in a week
and he's gotta go.
He'll try her over at one of her girlfriends.
Says that he's happier than he's ever been,
then hangs up.

And I'm caught, thinking
pounding inside, and sweating
nestled in the impression
this girl makes on me.

Picture

A picture of my Grandmother,
this woman I never knew.
Taken at a retirement home in Belfast.
Smiling by the window in her room.
It is dark outside,
a television is going, noticeable
almost distracting in the background.
She's frail and hunched in her wheel chair,
paralyzed I'm told, on her left side
by a stroke. Yet,
smiling for the camera.
Not wanting to, this I can see
but trying to give something.
Understanding, that someday a stranger
may ask about her, and when shown,
he'd see in this picture a woman
stronger than himself,
or anyone he knows.

Low

Down so low,
that you turn away the milk carton
with the face of the missing child on it.

Down so low,
that you don't care if your bread is stale
and your wine is discount.

That your favorite fish take-out closed
cause of all the shit in the bay.
That your T-shirt has holes under the arms.

Down so low,
that you're tired of lottery tickets.
Of landlords.
Even Jazz.

Tired of the want ads.
A toilet clogged with dead paper,
that ain't coming back.

Down so low,
that you're trying to hide.
Trying to pull the sheet over your head.
Just too low to lie down.

Down so low,
you know you're lucky to be alive.
Cause it's times like this when you die.
Down low enough to get hit by a bus
or shot in a drive by.

Down so low,
that low is on a roll,
you can feel it
and it's got you beat.

Rituals

A slow typewriter and coffee.
Smoke rings
and smoker's cough—
choke
gasp
exhale
chant—
the ritual.

Peeling away the wrapper on a bottle of beer
and thinking about "the story"
or
"the story" that when I have an idea
I'm gonna write.

But my mind is loaded as the ashtray
and I can't shake it.

As you go away, in my mind
I'm always dancing with you.
I know I wasted years searching
and all this time I was tripping over it—

I should have sent you love letters everyday,
in my tangled thoughts, I always did.

Smoke rings, smoker's cough,
a slow typewriter and coffee...

Fish

We need to talk.
She calls me from work,
to tell me this. And I listen,
because it's her phone
that I have my ear to.
Her apartment.
Her eggs I ate
for breakfast.
I know what's coming,
things have been going good lately.
Too good, she thinks.
So there's this need to talk.
We talk everyday, I say,
sometimes twice, when we have
something to say.
Dead fucking silence
That's not good enough, she says
We need . . .
need to . . . "communicate more."
She tells me to stop laughing.
And then makes her point!
I assure her I'm working on it.
But she continues,
everybody knows, communication
is the basis of any good relationship.

Who knows? Cosmopolitan.
Your divorced sister.
That guy at work that
wants to screw you?

I am a good fish.

Now we have a reason,
to stay on the phone a while longer.

And there will be tears
about this talk.
Apologies.
It will take some B.S.
till we come around,
and say our, "I Love You's."
Laugh a little.
Describe our days so far,
say, "I Love You" again.
And tonight, we'll make love
like Salmon,
and things will be better,
because there won't be
all good between us.

On my back, on the floor

Giant gaps in the Venetian blinds
at this place.
Shadows from table umbrellas passing
by my walls.
The sun hanging by a noose,
about to be dropped.

Pictures of people and dogs.

Doors that are French.
Aqua pools and open courtyards.
Owls in palm trees,
waiting for the cat opera to begin.

i am shifting from sunshine
to a cave
i could be a leaf hidden in the pages
of this book
my clothes are hanging on the floor

i am alive

Influences

People like us
we're not supposed
to step on a stage
write a book
or play a note.
We get threatened
because we have a thought.
Fear of moving off track,
being out of the balance
or falling in love.
We're meant to believe
we should go through life
only to cause
the least possible damage.
Keepers of the pond,
simply wading
in waters of mediocrity.
Afraid to vision or swim.
Drowning,
splashing about
without hope of resurfacing.

Well. Fuck That—

Never be stale, man. Or subtle.
Let go of reason, cause
the rules you've cherished
have passed with the night.
Lose your mind, waste a little time.
Fish at midnight.
Let the worm eat at your heart awhile
and don't worry about your purpose—
Ghandi had a purpose. MLK the same.
We have none.

Only chariots need a guide.

So look beyond the dark
see through the truth
and when you do
let the poet make the gesture on his own
because sometimes laughter
is better than crying.
Just sit back, in the beauty of words
and wait for good dreams,
for only in the listless drift
will you find the secret value
of swinging with the angels.

Apotheosis

You're out on your girl.
The one that's been good to you.
The one that takes care of you
and reminds you of who you are.
Calls and tells you, she loves you
and that makes you forget you were
getting ready to jump off the roof.

But you're out on this girl
because the one next to you
has bigger tits.
So you're putting up
and looking out the window.
Doing Cuervo shots and nodding alot
to all the nothing she has to say.

You want to go, but you want her.
So you shake more hands
and watch as she kisses more cheeks.
Fake interest and hide disinterest
in whatever's being said to you.
Trying to think about what you'll get later
and wondering if it's worth what you feel
now.

Then it comes, in the middle of this miasma—
you have a thought
and it flattens you, you realize
you're just a jerk.

Like Love

The road is like a stream, the Hog
flowing like a lost oar in the asphalt current.

Long, tan fingers, used to picking at Cobb salads
at the country club, playing with the Marlboros in my
pocket.
Clinging to the leather about my waist as might
a gourmet minx.

The noontide light passing through the rib cage
of Joshua Trees; like morning for Matisse.

Laughing off fear at the back of my neck,
whispering things that are lost in the dry wind.

Convenience stores staining the desert landscape —
tombstones along some scenic forest lawn.

And for a single moment, while the sound is down low,
I think you know why I do the things I do.
Why there is no job to hold down, a car payment
to make, even, why your father hates me,
and you're with me.

Scenes of strawberries, across crisp farmland.

Leaving the road at some exit that doesn't
even have a sign announcing it. A still night.
Making love on a blanket by a well.
Afterwards, talking about cats and an old movie
you saw last night, shooting stars and your brother
in Canada. Drinking wine and just being
there under blankets, never making it to the place.
And somewhere in Elysium I think,
this must be almost like love.

Icarus passes by in the moonlight.

Problems

You don't understand,
that your problems,
those little things
that you have
and tell me, don't mean anything.
In one ear—
you know the rest.
Look at me,
How can I know,
about tummy tucks
and Tofu hot dogs
and the new
Hollywood Bowl season?
All these things,
I know nothing about,
yet, for some reason
you tell me anyway.
Just come home from work
and start in.
And then get mad,
when I look
out the window,
at the night
instead of at you,
and your problems.
But I know,
you'll only be satisfied
if I listen,
with little to offer,
but sitting still
and taking the time
to see
where you stand.

The Howard Johnson's World Tour Poem

I remember
    a motel room in Santa Fe.
Children Welcome.   Pets allowed.
     —We felt we were covered—
                 STONED
and watching Sesame Street.
       LEARNING
from Big Bird.   Jim Henson, somewhere, probably
PISSED.
                  The Impala
OVERHEATED in the parking lot.
Jimi Hendrix   stuck   in the tapedeck.
No Beer
    and those two cartoons of cigarettes
                                    ???
          AAA TOUR BOOK — missing
same as the maps.   <u>No</u> alarm clock.
      (clocks never let you finish your dreams)

                       That copy,
of *Fear and Loathing in Las Vegas*, left behind
         on some picnic table outside Norman, OK.
Nothing   to read and pissed.
So Eddie
     BROKE
       that suit rack
     to get at the theft proof hangers.

PROVED NOTHING
                  While I
    pondered the signs in the bathroom awhile.

Do <u>NOT</u> Flush cans, cigarettes or baby diapers.
     D
     0
     W
     N
        the TOILET.
                —Only tried the cans.
So I sit, clogged toilet and all.
                 But
     I'm <u>NOT</u> Crazy.
(no matter what you say) I still have
control   of
           ALL my faculties.
Just rethinking life   and waiting. I
remember so I've changed.   But who cares?
                   Cause
things are bad
        and getting no
easier.
     So I still keep IT around. Something
I've had too long
But it takes me back
        to a time
          when I was laughing
           or high.
I   n   e   e   d   t   h   a   t   n   o w.
When I'm trying to bear it
        and go on
      rather
    than push about blindly.
What I'm saying is,
   do you FEEL what I feel
        ?
          ?

The need
        to sit
        alone
        in some
                restaurant and just remember that,
"We are <u>NOT</u> doomed"
        (I mean most of us are close)
                                    But...
God may smile on an honest

                                    bartender.
Maybe someone who found

                        a box of cats
        and cared for them.
                        A
                good   mechanic
                                may be spared.
        This is comforting I think.
So   I yell   to Eddie
        "Tell   Jimi   to
just hang on...   we're coming"
        And I emerge
                        WISHING
I didn't know   as much (which is nothing)
                        but
        able   to   swallow   the ache
FORGET   another   DAY
        and just get back
                    on the PATH.

Places Where I've Slept

In Boise.
In a Studebaker.
A lot of cars I can't remember.
In an alley near Dodger Stadium.
On a couch in a hospital.
On a beach in Miami, where I was arrested.
In a Miami jail.
In a sleeping bag on the front lawn of a girl
I had just met. *Her father turned the sprinklers on me.*
On a hammock in someone's backyard that
I didn't think was home. *They were.*
In an all night Donut Shop in Vegas.
In an office I was painting.
On a beach in Ensenada, where someone stole my shoes.
In a hotel in Palm Springs that had
a phone in the bathroom.
In the projection booth of a movie theater
a job that lasted one night.
Underneath a playground slide while it rained.
In the dugout of some minor league field in St. Petersburg.
Not on Doug's fishing boat.
In the booth of a Taco Bell where my girlfriend worked.
In a bus station in Oakland where I sat and slept
and waited to fall asleep some more.

Bob Dylan

Sounds,
like
gunshots
and ambulance
sirens.
Someone
going through
a
trash can.
Want sounds.
Sometimes screams.
Nighttime sounds
at noon
and
harmonica blues
past
midnight.
Bleeding,
one cigarette
into another
sounds.
Purple sunsets
on
Mars.
The sound
of
dreams.
Donut shop
sounds
and
Bob Dylan's
voice.
Sounds,
listen
before the
ear
is parch.

Thanksgiving Day 1989

I know a poem
should say something more
than I smoked
two packs of Camels
on Venice beach today.
Drank some Coronas,
and ate a pack
of Oscar Meyer Bologna.
But lying low and still
in the dark,
underneath my serape,
avoiding the cop
that walks the boardwalk,
I can't think what —

Knowing, that I only
know this place
and never caring
if I ever get to *that* point.
And then, these books
written by the ones
they call our contemporaries.
Do any of them amount to more
than just a few lines of Bukowski?
That's what I'm thinking of tonight,
drunk on Venice beach
dreamy and still.

Pacific Standard Time

this toilet
with it's creaky flush
—a little dribble—
and it's happy-go-lucky waste
clinging
to the side of the porcelain
hoping, never to be discovered
or wiped clean.
this toilet
where nothing really goes down
even when you "jimmy" the handle
or bully the plunger
it remains unmoving; shitstained
and clogged—festering
with ambitious notions.
this toilet
it is where you have to go
if you end up wanting to be
in the thing.
this toilet
with it's blue-blue dreams
and wide eyed discharge—
the only thing changing
is the water.

Deadline
for J.A.

Angel eyes and takes giant steps
Graceful; like a moth in water
Swaying, then crumbling down like night
—while even palm trees lay still
And moonbeams tarnish inspite
Of Charlotte's many webs.

Then this ark too will pass—
From clever dingy to leaky tub
Leaving behind no more utterances for yesterday
An oath for that dawning—between us
When the rot sets in ; take it away, lover
In your spirit laughter, as mine goes adrift.

Trailer Man

The night out my window
is beautiful.
A full moon, lots of stars.
The sky, not quite black
more grey or deep blue
like the colors of industry.
It meets the water
somewhere in the distance.
Sitting in the pitch, it reminds me
of something by Carver
and for a moment I think I know—
But then she flushes
and the whole trailer rocks,
the pipes echo throughout, deep
like indigestion or a chainsaw.
And while the walls mumble, the bathroom door
swings open with a shriek
and it is lost.
I retreat,
returning to Jack and the Camel
by the pyramid and the palm trees.
And I am reminded that I am not happy,
there is no reason for a smile.
I am a shadow on the Sequoias,
the moon shits on me.
Looking at her,
I want to take away the heartache
I've given someone, but then I wise up—
I am not well enough to fight.

Tequila and Lime

You carry heaven and hell with you.
—Sri Ramana Maharshi

No Inspiration
no heart, no balls.
Gutless,
drained and empty
with nothing to say.
Smoking
frail and pathetic,
ash
and the smell of booze.
Tequila and Lime.
Drink rings, smoke rings
and spills.
Some puke.
Unshaven, greasy and angry
but with nothing left to say.
So fuck you
I never made any promises
and life ain't no apology.
This chapter is closed—a done gig.
Go away and leave me alone,
sweaty with blood on my fingers
listless and afraid.
And don't look back, don't even think about it
cause this last one wasn't even any good.

TWO

To know that nothing matters after all.
To know there's no real difference
between the rich and the poor.
To know that eternity is neither drunk
nor sober, to know it young and be a poet.

Skid Row Wine - Kerouac

Daedalus is Dead

You never thought it would come at night
and you scratch your unshaven face and
consider the fact that you never looked
at the sun today. And even though
the dryness of the evening makes you sweat,
you can feel the rain as you always do
and with this you gesture forward and
whisper, there will be pain as promised
but her eyes shine and she says,
"God is a crying man." She laughs silly.

You look at your watch and ask her
if she wants to go, but she shakes her
head from side to side, her jewelry rattles
when she does it, and you imitate her
and laugh when you look at her colorless
face and realize you didn't want to go anyway.
You feel cheerless when you consider
all the drunken nights when you concluded
that being "in the act" was the only way
to pass, but somehow, when it's here
that thought makes you weary, as if
you were a passenger whose abandoned
a sinking ship, waiting to drown in the pitch,
yet worried about where the luggage might be.

A Waiter is in front of you and the two of them
are laughing as lovers might. You are
surprised since you thought everyone
had gone and he tells you that there
will be no more food and you say
that is fine and order another bottle.
She asks him why he is still here

and he says it is his work and
that he's glad it's over and looks at his
watch and says, not long now and
you repeat, not long now, and then
he disappears down some stairs behind
the kitchen counter and you never see him again.

Ask me something she says.
        (Beat)
- Why do I brush my teeth till I see
  blood in the sink?
- No good. My turn. When do little boys
  stop letting their pants fall to the floor
  when they go to the bathroom?
- Who says they stop? My turn.
  Do you like birds?
- Not the ones that talk, but the ones
  that crack nuts in their beak. Me again?
        (Beat)
  What's it going to be like?

You sit back, look through your wine
and think; like the telescopes on the pier
when the money's gone. SNAP!
And it goes black.

The Cook walks out from behind the open grill.
He looks old, short, heavy and he wipes
his hands on the front of his apron often.
He looks at his watch and then at you and
smiles. He is in no hurry.
His back is to you now, at a dimly
lit table at the rear of the place.
You watch as he lights a candle, pours
some wine, and begins to carve up
octopus slices into small pieces.

a braid of ash colored grease where his
hair vanishes halfway up his ample, round
head. He takes a drink and you are reminded
of Socrates, but then you look at her
and she's staring into a fireplace retaining
three unlit logs in it's den and she asks
you, without lifting her eyes, if you'd rather
be stranded in the desert or the Arctic
not having food or water and that seems
to change everything. You never thought
it would be like this.

You can remember writing a paper in
college in which you were asked to imagine
this. You wrote a story about how you'd
go to the beach and paddle out on your
board beyond the swell and just sit and watch
it happen. When your paper came back
it was covered in red ink and you were
told that the work was poetic yet vague but
traffic would be so congested that you'd never
make it to the waves on time.
And his comments made you smile but
after that you never thought about it again.

Music is coming from far away and she
says it's strange but the man who made
this song was blind and you don't recognize
it but you ask her if she reads Yeats
anyway and she nods and you ask her
to dance. You move to the center of the
room, where you pick up some chairs and
a table so there is some space and when
you take her hand you can feel the blush
of her palms and you look into her steady eyes
and sway to the slow, sad notes.

You can feel the warmth of her ear against
your cheek as you try to think of children
and what they might be doing now, but
you can't and instead you think of your mother
and remember how nice she smelled when
you'd visit her after school while she worked
the perfume counter at Bloomingdales.
She'd tell you that you couldn't stay and
give you the money to go to the movie theatre
on Seventh, and afterwards you and your
friends would take the subway to 153rd St. and try
to knock over tombstones in St. Michael's Cemetery.
The thought fades slowly with the music,
and you hold tight; if you knew her name
you'd say it in your prayers.

Twilight passes but you don't stop the dance
and the only light is the candle burning
at the table where the old, short, heavy
cook sits. He's taken off his apron and
is staring at a black and white photograph
of a boy in shorts standing by the sea that he's taken
down off the wall. And you watch as he
slowly smothers the flame of the candle with
his thumb and forefinger and in the eclipse
you hear him say that he'd wish to lodge
a complaint. And then he is quiet.

Your heart is moving your tongue and you're
content with the warmth of not having to
say anything. You look out an open window
and see the moon and but one star in the sky
and you realize you can finally be content
with the message you left on your answering machine.

Not long now you think...

Lies

A cuffing. Come here, I'm going to give you
a good cuffing were his words.

Come out of the bathroom later to get some ice,
crying, with a red ear.

Sometimes two. Thankful there only is that many.
Upset, because ears couldn't be a nose.

Trying to hide them in school that day with a cap.
Long hair would have been best.

A haircut. Come here, so I can give you
a good cut before they call you a "Sheila," were his words.

Keeping the ears clear for an accurate cuffing.
Every two weeks in the garage.

Heavy nerves and rusty scissors, bad light
and thin hair.

Cuffings and haircuts and red ears that wouldn't go away.
Things, to make up lies about for those who asked.

X.

She has been stripped
pawed at
opened
and drained.

Hollowed and misguided now
like one of the rest.

Long legs and low soul.
For someone who could not swim,
she found her maximum depth
in this place.

23

Went back to the old place
after being on the road for a time.
Ran into my friend Steve
and I was glad to see him.
Asked him if he wanted to go grab a beer.
Get shit faced—
do stuff like when we were sixteen.
End up at a place
with flashing neon on top of it
XXX   XXX   XXX
If that's not good,
maybe meet some girls,
who don't care if we have money
or not. Who knows?
Just drive all night.
Find the border, like old times.
But, he wasn't interested,
and went on about his business.
Said it was a Tuesday night.
"Tuesday night," as in having to be at work
on Wednesday morning.
And I laughed, but he was finished.
So I hassled him,
like we'd done to each other for years.
Said he was weak.
Told him to get out of this rut.
He got pissed.
Looked me over
from hair to high tops
and then let it fly.
Just cause I'm not doing
nothing with my life,
I shouldn't get on him
for doing something with his.

"Not doing nothing," that's funny.
He teaches kindergarten.
And, he likes this rut.
The rut is important.
But I'm doing nothing.
Struggling is nothing, I guess.
So is getting by. Nothing.
But when you think about it,
just being twenty three
is doing nothing. No matter.

One Year Drunk

One Year Of   Advil . . . pissing on walls
. . . being down . . . sunglasses . . . Jazz
. . . getting high . . . wandering . . . being cold
. . . getting evicted . . . getting thrown around
. . . spitting . . . thinking . . . passing out
selling out . . . puking . . . losing jobs . . .
falling down . . . finding jobs . . . losing friends
. . . sleeping in . . . singing loud . . . being sick . . .
fighting . . . love . . . filling ashtrays . . .
crashing cars . . . bad breath . . . strange beds
. . . going to the movies . . . blindness . . . cops
lying on the beach . . . laughing and crying . . .
nights . . . newspapers . . . *Past*.

Everyone

Everyone
goes fast
wants an introduction
falls in love,
wishes they hadn't.

Everyone
is vague
efficient in their
use of canvas
steals,
wants.

Everyone
merges,
loiters
makes due,
waits for the new model.

Everyone
needs a meal
needs a kleenex
has a place
that looks like the Grinch
has been there.

Everyone
hides
knows the bleeding.
Hustles,
and is never recognized.

Remembering Green and Blue Things

They'll ask us to tell them about
the stumps and the sky.
A time, when dolphins didn't lie on rocks;
a time when all of it was avoidable.

And we'll dribble on and on, in our passing
ways, about a time when it <u>was</u> something
to serve your country and what it meant
to get with an aerobics instructor or stewardess—
Not unlike the ones before us
who could remember McKinley and free coffee
and fulfilling their morphine kick
at the corner drugstore without
a prescription.

And we'll blah, blah, blah, about those days so much,
they'll finally have to tell us to go straight to hell.

D.C.

When business is bad,

the vendors,

use stale pretzels

to power their carts.

The Thing

When you're nineteen
you just don't believe—
so you have faith
in the thing.
When you're nineteen,
everybody has a thing.

When he was nineteen,
my oldest brother just drank.
J.D. was his thing.
Two days after his nineteenth birthday,
my other brother joined the army -
He had this fighting thing.

My other brother's thing
reminded my Dad of his.
A place called Da Nang.
He was that age.
He saw his best friend step on a live mine.
That would always be my Dad's thing.

While my Dad was in Vietnam,
my Mom watched T.V. and waited.
That's all she did, she says.
Two things.
She wouldn't tell me how old she was
when she did her things.

My sister got married at nineteen,
to an older guy from Seattle.
She spent a lot of time planning a wedding.
Getting a church and a hall, picking
bridesmaids and napkins and stuff.
Her thing lasted ten months.

She found the guy from Seattle,
getting blown by his secretary
in some filing room at the place
where he worked.
My sister said he looked happy.
I guess that was his thing.

When I was nineteen,
I didn't know nothing.
Didn't even know my thing.
Which I guess, knowing that you
know nothing is your thing.

Since then, things have only got worse.

beat

it's that beat
beat that makes you
drag on all the things
they like
beat makes it hard
to listen when they
talk about their stuff
cause beat doesn't tie-up
your money or your time
beat can't swim
so it drowns
in the mediocrity
in which they wade
and that makes it hard
for them to see beyond
their shit
beat may be suffering
but it's the matter
that will make you weary
that's the beauty, man
beat keeps you alive
lets you ditch work
to spend some time in a park
just sitting with squirrels
the raw
the poetic and the vague
all beat
pays only one bill
and that's what allows you
to look at them
and go on
not hate and fall back
as they do you.

brutus in his hat

pigeons mobilized against the soggy bread.
unclear days and too much silence. boarded
rooms. everywhere. do we know our influences?
the moon and the tide. pressure. we don't
see autumn anymore. **autumn is lost.** sleep
late on sunday morning but forget to dream.
dreams are like autumn. and excuses. hearing
birds in a tree, till one falls. feeling guilty
about spending the afternoon in a movie
theatre. when was the last time you heard
the word autumn? **bayer knows heroin.**
alone and nowhere to fall back. falling hard. let
giants sleep they say. waiting for the waitress
to come back and listening to people talk about
getting what they want. **cassiopeia is the
W and libra is a kite.** these times.
can we borrow some hope somewhere or is this
the way it will be forever? "Aquarius, that's all."
the woman peeling potatoes. storm front moving
in. **are you desperate enough**? do you know
what you want? the old woman drinking milk from
the cat dish. **dogs and leash laws.** the doctor's
favorite words are frail and lean. hang ups.
the man that reads the paper at breakfast. thoughts
passing me like brutus in his hat.

February

Willing to start clean. Lie.
Lose It. Spend the time
scrambling, to get it back.

Looking through a T.V. screen,
waiting for commercials.
Cynical now, and original.

Tearing up all those things
you wrote when your pen
was just sad and ugly.

Waiting for nothing to come on,
flicking back and forth between three stations,
needing more than that New Year's resolution.

Mad Dog of the Neighborhood

She sent me next door
to straighten out our neighbor
the one with the dog that
tramples her roses
When I met him I told him
I didn't want any trouble
Had his dog been out lately?
No he said
At that moment
from behind me
I hear a dog running up my
neighbor's yard,
ducks past me into the house
tail wagging
Sorry my neighbor said
it won't happen again
Offered me a beer
The next morning I went to get my paper
fed upon at both ends
The garbage knocked over
And it went on like this
Shit on the roses
A fishing pole chewed in two
Plastic handles on some tools I'd left out
gnawed all to hell
Laundry that usually hangs on the line
pulled to the ground
My wife was irate
And we weren't the only victims
Every morning someone from the neighborhood
was standing next door
Complaining
The neighbors even seemed mad at us
for being our neighbor's neighbor

Then one day it just stopped
The garbage
the newspaper found peace
No barking
The roses grew
My wife was happy again
I forgot all about my neighbor
till one day later that Fall
while fixing a cabinet door
I reached for my hammer
gripped the roughness of the gnawed handle
and remembered the day when
that dog came bounding up behind me
tail wagging
so full of life.

Order

Order is locked is control is perverse

a plight so dizzying so wrong it drains

it kills it's out so spin and shout

and fall and hurt feel heat and wine

see sunset see moons drip peace and stay afloat

with dance be life be high so free

so pure find vision find hope hold truth

hold on and create mystify us with need

and control them with your Disorder.

Advice

The old man had lots of advice about women

He'd stay up nights
watching old movies and in the morning
he might say, "That Cleopatra was a real hussy,
watch out for her type, boy"

He was always warning me about women.

I'd help him wash the car on Sunday.
He'd be telling me how mornings were
best for washing cars, then he'd stop, say
"Never marry one of those hand models"

"A hand model?"
"You know, a girl who gets her picture taken
holding things. Stay away from that type."

Strange, cause Mom was a nurse.

Sometime after we washed that car,
he left us. The nurse and I.
Just left, and there was no one there
to walk me through it when I did meet Cleopatra
and the hand model.

All this crap Is getting me down

All this crap is getting me down my friend said
I'm studying the invisible universe you know
for the government
Shit you wouldn't understand (no one does)
That's why I finally had to give away the family car
the Cadillac
too much goddamn trouble
Just parked and left it with the key in the ignition
The wife made me promise to put the next one in her name
Wants it in writing
Can you believe that?
Can you blame her?
Look at me!
I know I look good
You know why ?
Cause I run to work everyday
No car
Of course I can't tell you where work is
Government stuff
I started to paint the house
red and green for Christmas
The creatures got a kick out of that
He calls his kids creatures.
But I ran out of paint
when I went to get more
the news came on T.V.
goddamn place is getting me so down
you know what I'm going to do
Do you know?
I'm going to get one of those Harley Davidsons
you know like you have
I'm going to ride across country
and talk to all these industry big shots
all the cities
Get us out of this depression we're in

Show them the way
Do you want to go hunting tomorrow?
I forgot you don't hunt
My friend goes into the woods
shoots his .22 at rocks and ducks the ricochet.
Well if we don't go hunting
maybe I'll go to Australia
That's if I can get the time off work
Just sit on the beach
Count clouds
I think that's what I need
When things get you down
go back to what you know
Remember that?
Wheel me back to the room
I'm gonna get some sleep
All this stuff makes me tired
I hope it's not time for the goddamn news
Get's me so down, you know
If only you knew what I'm working on
Government stuff

Elected Man

When he farts
low and hollow
into the soft leather,
he hears the cries
of a million hungry children —
                      He answers the phone.

Crowds

This crowd that lives above me
to them I'm just the guy
with the books and the sax—
just figure I can't afford anything
more than T-shirts and jeans
but they like me to fix their cars
when they have trouble.
They think a guy who's home every afternoon
must know something about engines.
Cause they wear nice suits,
but the lot of them couldn't fix a flat.
One of them pays me twenty every other month
to change the oil.
Says he's lost without the manual,
which disappeared.

The guys like to tease me about my girlfriend
cause they recognize her from a porn film.
They leer from behind curtains
and watch her skirt ride up her ass
when she climbs on my motorcycle.
Right after they'll call the police
and complain that our parties are too loud.
Leer some more when the cops
come out and roust us.
Deny the involvement to my face the next day.
The guys like games.

Their wives don't like my friend Carl
cause he lost his hands in Vietnam.
They call him scary when they huddle
in the laundry room in the mornings.
Complain to one another about how
they have to leave their porches and run inside
when we sit out and play our Congo drums

in the sun.
And when they hear us laughing,
they get all bent,
assume we're making fun of them
cause they shop at a place
called Brooks Brothers.
They don't understand,
we're just glancing through their manuals.

Jazz Poem

"Wrong notes are all right"
—Ornette Coleman

Getting drunk and getting headaches.
Nicotine haze.

Fights with greedy blue eyes.
A hold on the bleeding.

Pond at his eyes.
The run-off.

Nights in taxi cabs and subways.
Morning in The Projects.

Blowin' horn in the spotlight.
Breaking tools and broken.

Sweat and sex and nine ball.
Christ at the Wurlitzer.

Searching and forgetting intervals.
The shape of things to come.

A Good Time to Lose Your Girlfriend

You know nothing about cars,
as you pop the hood, and the
steam making factory underneath
goes to work, generating the white fog
that's hot about your face.

You walk around the engine often though,
looking, touching things
with your shirt off.
"Piece of shit," you say alot.

And inside,
she doesn't hear you say,
"try the engine now."

Her head resting against the window,
thinking, that a Porsche
would never overheat in the desert.
Never.

Always

Always drunk,
when you need breakfast.
Spend change on eggs,
not liquor.

Always bloody,
after a fight with her new boyfriend.
Cause he hits her and she calls you.
He's bigger.

Always dandruff,
in your hair
when you think about all the money you owed,
long ago.

Always cold,
underneath Santa Monica Pier,
when you talk about the highways on the moon
and everybody laughs.

Always clean underwear on your birthday.

Girl

She doesn't even want to be with him
but she kisses him anyway
cause she's drunk, right?
And sometime later, at someone's apartment,
they make love (or fuck), whatever.
And it feels the same as all the others.
The smell of his sweat,
the rapidness of his tongue,
preservation of the menthol cigarettes
he nervously smoked all night.

Painless, she thinks,
while it's happening and
impassive when he leaves
realizing she knows nothing about him.
Resting instead, hands on her stomach,
thinking about the boy
from a couple of months ago.
The one she brought in
and told things to.
About an abortion,
her parents split
her mom's boyfriends
and her dad's wives.
Told these things,
while crying next to him in bed,
and his body was still.
Which seems strange now.
The one whose lips seemed different.

Then SNAP
it's passed,
and she's back to hoping that
she'll never see him again.

Boy

He senses,
she wants
to believe in him
so bad,
that he lies,
about everything.
At first,
it's just
to get her into bed,
but later,
he'll want her
to fall in love with him.
So he creates,
the people he knows
the places he's been
cars he's driven,
anything that comes up.
And at the end of the night
he grabs the bar tab
to verify something,
for now, he knows
things are forged.
So sometime later,
when he slips up
and she catches him,
it will be too late
and they'll be stuck with it.
Until, he has nothing left
to lie about,
and then
it will be time
to move on.

poem 37

i talk to myself too much here,
                    look upward often
                              let the eyes drool.

are you there with your mom today?
maybe having some good tea together?

it is not in mirrors i see you now
or in clouds, as some say
but most often
                    when i am near water
the ocean,
          or standing in rain;
          passing time in still pools
i do not talk to myself with water
—the mind slows—instead i am given thoughts;

     you remain the few good things i am.

but i would let them all go
                    for just one cup of Darjeeling
                              with you
                                   on this day.

                              may 11, 1997

afternoons

Drunk.
And Stoned.
Takin' Blues
and playing checkers.

Just thinking that someday
I may want to live forever.

Meet George Best*

Never been a pretty poet—
                    wish I was.
Beautiful like Bukowski
                    or Baudelaire.
I look at their words and realize,
                        mine are starving.
That sometimes when I speak,
                        it is just drool—
and that with the thoughts of God;
there are always those of a girl,
                        in a white silk bra.
What can I do?
                    —metaphor is not my friend.
And syntax?
                    —syntax generally shits on me.

I had thoughts of being, something like,
the George Best of all this.
But I realize I have no gift. No capacity.
Just some moments —these wounds and caterwauls—
                    scribbled from time to time,
on a napkin or a shirtsleeve.
                        Insignificant, I know
as the moths I watch out my window
who have strokes in blue light, as I write this.
And like lifeless drones, these pages too, could
just as easily fall through the cracks in my neighbor's
porch, as end up on this spine.
But they are all that is left.
                    I had wanted better for us.

If you have read this far and are pissed
you're not alone—
cause' I've seen some of them myself in print
and I wanted to drink till I threw.
Apologize. Then run away,
                              faster than rain.
Oh, like a dog, I will tell you;
the best thing I ever thought I wrote
was once described by someone I respected,
as being that which was, "less than good."
She was more than right.

Maybe there should be a warning in front
—like a pack of Chesterfield's
but it has become too much too think about now
and as usual the words do not come...

A fetus' head is attached to it's heart in the womb

These moments —some wounds—
                    all that is left,
scribbled from time to time,
                    on a napkin or shirtsleeve.
metaphor is still not my friend—

A fetus' head is attached to it's heart in the womb.

              And I have come undone.

*George Best played soccer for Manchester United at
  the age of seventeen. He is from Northern Ireland.

Drain and Baggage

You drop me.
Make my heart stop, skip
                              sink.

Deep
in the sounds of running water
I hear your voice
soft and hollow
like whispers that exit
till I shut the tap
and then, in the soft drip
sometimes screams.

My heart has changed
from red to blue to black
                              and back—
You see, I've swallowed the ache
dropped out and held on—
closed the blinds on the city
and through the uneven drapes
looked out on the telephone poles
on the hills at sunset
said a prayer for dead hearts
and past loves.

You took sweet dreams
and gave back nightmares—
Things that bury me, haunt me,
                              embrace me.
Because there are no substitutes for holding
in the pain. No excuses for walking in
on your lover in the act or taking
a needle in the arm.

Yes, you drop me
but in the end you'll miss this,
cause all that you stood for is gone.
Just tequila down the throat
or piss down a urinal.
And the sinking will pass.
Pass,
like a lie that has been sorted
out for you, or a brother
who is now a stranger.

Tantalus

Silver and white balloons
traveling over my head.
From a place,
where people are laughing
and shaking hands.
Conducting themselves,
in a proper fashion.
A wedding or a birthday maybe.
Something that could be called
a "function." Balloons,
from a place where they probably
wouldn't want someone like me.
A place where I'd start coughing
during speeches or introductions.
Not even able to hold it,
until they finished their talks
and begin clapping.
Yes, balloons from a place where
people applaud one another.
But I'll just sit here,
on this bench, in this place
where I sat yesterday.
Alone, with the thoughts
that get away. Knowing only,
that you don't need me, anymore.

last call

"A severe insult to the brain."
—Doctors at St. Vincent Hospital
on what killed Dylan Thomas

the smell of bleach,
     with a feces twist.
amongst the good filth above the urinal
     — an image coming back —
GHOSTLIKE
     on mint green tile and bathing
          in 60 watts of yellow light—
for a single moment,
     my shadow; then
          just a leonard cohen smudge.

"you don't have to go home but you can't stay here"

          hiss. closing time.
i tip my weight,
          all tobasco and attitude.
     knocking comes.
i will wait it out.   i will not emerge
     until i know who i am.
there is something on my pants,
          i will not touch it.
who am i?
     gene vincent . jeff koons . peter north.
three wise men...
     i feel my liver quiver,
like flames
     on the last day of earth—
who am i?

Someone who never had a good opening line—
"Hey, Hercules killed his whole family."
maybe someone who has lived   too long himself.
     someone,
who should begin digging his own hole.
     i shake it out.
     i could just as easily be
the ice plant at the side of the road,
     or a thief like everyone i know.
i was the kid
     with perfect attendance
     in sunday school.
oh, where's your god now moses?
     bookers. bakers. and makers mark.
why are these flies in my ear?
     who am i?
just a guy who wants another drink.
     — i'm not afraid of commitment.
just a guy who doesn't feel much for himself;
whose soul remains both clunky and vile,
     insane but the same—
     hanging on
breathing like someone next to me.
     keep working.   keep the cable on.
know the truth will always hurt you.

     i am tired
     wounded, drowning
     who am i?

"you're closing out your bar tab, that's <u>who</u> you are!"

they told me what to say,
                and how to say it.
where to stand.
now my days are given
                to drawing shadows on the sun
and dreaming in negative.
it's like the scene in *raging bull*
where la motta goes:

   "you never put me down ray, you never put me down."

I feel it now,
stutter breath and gesture;
pick a cig up off that gravestone.
    you can't always bury a dead man.
                      i think but get lost—
then the smudge comes through
    for me again;
                in a room full of real people,
                you are four toes —

                       saludé.

For information on this or other books from
The Bowery Press, please contact:

Lost Poets Productions
5750 Wilshire Blvd.
Suite 580
Los Angeles, CA 90036

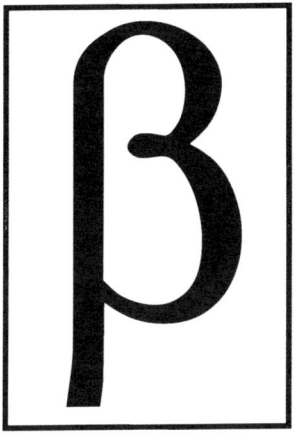

NEW YORK, NEW YORK